THE PASSIVE PATH TO PROSPERITY

Master Financial Independence
In 3 Years Or Less

JEFFREY S LOOMIS

Copyright

Copyright © by Jeffrey S. Loomis 2024. All rights reserved. Before this document is duplicated or reproduced in any manner, the publisher's consent must be gained. Therefore, the contents within can neither be stored electronically, transferred, nor kept in a database. Neither in Part nor full can the document be copied, scanned, faxed, or retained without approval from the publisher or creator.

Table of Contents

Copyright...1
Table of Contents..2
Dedication.. 4
Introduction...6
Understanding Passive Income............................. 10
Types of Passive Income Streams............................12
Myths and Realities of Passive Income...................17
Reality Of Passive Income.......................................19
Leveraging Inflation.. 23
Your Secret Weapon..23
Turning Inflation into Opportunity............................ 26
Inflation-Proof Investments...................................... 28
Adapting Strategies in an Inflationary Economy.....32
Setting Financial Goals for Independence...............36
Short-Term vs. Long-Term Goals............................. 38
Tracking Progress and Adjusting Plans...................41
Celebrating Milestones Along the Way.................... 43
Budgeting for Success... 46
Eliminating Debt Efficiently...................................... 48
Creating an Emergency Fund..................................50
The Importance of Financial Literacy......................53
EXPLORING INVESTMENT OPPORTUNITIES...........55
Practical Tips for Beginners..................................... 62
Common Mistakes to Avoid......................................65
Real Estate Investments.. 67

Investment Strategies... 72
Key Considerations... 74
Peer-to-Peer Lending.. 76
How Peer-to-Peer Lending Works............................. 78
Benefits of Peer-to-Peer Lending.............................. 81
Risks and Considerations.. 82
Getting Started with Peer-to-Peer Lending............... 85
Diversifying Your Portfolio... 87
CREATING MULTIPLE INCOME STREAMS............ 90
Identifying Potential Income Sources....................... 91
Balancing Active and Passive Income...................... 93
Scaling Your Income Streams.................................... 95
Letting Your Money Work for You.............................. 98
Conclusion... 100
7...101
Harnessing the Power of Technology..................... 101
Digital Tools for Passive Income............................. 102
Online Business Models... 106
Cryptocurrency and Blockchain Opportunities..... 109
STAYING AHEAD IN A DIGITAL WORLD................ 113
Overcoming Challenges and Setbacks................... 117
Common Pitfalls and How to Avoid Them..............118
Learning from Financial Mistakes...........................120
Staying Motivated During Tough Times................. 122
Building Resilience and Adaptability..................... 125
Conclusion... 127
The Psychology of Wealth Building........................ 129
Habits' Significance for Financial Achievement....131

Visualization and Goal-Setting Techniques........... 134
The Impact of Community and Networking........... 137
Living Your Financially Independent Life............... 139
Giving Back.. 142
The Joy of Philanthropy...142
Planning for a Legacy.. 143
Continuous Growth and Learning......................... 146

Dedication

To my family, whose unwavering support and belief in my journey fueled my determination.

To my mentors and friends, who guided me with wisdom and encouragement along the way.

And to everyone seeking financial independence, may this book inspire you to take control of your future and achieve the freedom you deserve.

This is for all of you, who dream big and act boldly

Introduction

When I initially started in the real estate industry, I had no clue what I was getting into. Passive income felt like a pipe dream rather than a genuine possibility, with promises that were almost too good to be true. But like many of you, I was determined to make my own way out of the grind and live my life as I saw fit by being financially independent.

I'm Jeffrey S. Loomis, and I've been deeply involved in the real estate and passive income industries for the last ten years. The journey wasn't always simple; there were times when I doubted myself, obstacles that were overwhelming at the time, and setbacks that tried my willpower. I've dealt with everything from challenging tenants to market downturns. Still, through it all, I've discovered one vital lesson: with the correct tactics, achieving financial independence is not only conceivable but also attainable very quickly.

My first purchase was a little duplex that required more repairs than I had previously thought. I dedicated every free minute to repairing it, picking new skills along the way, often by making mistakes. Even though there were times when I wondered whether making the sacrifice was worthwhile, I persisted because I could see a day when money would serve me rather than the other way around. Eventually, the duplex served as the foundation for my financial independence. Before long, the money it brought in enabled me to buy other homes, each one taking me one step closer to my self-imposed target. I was able to live off the passive income from my assets for a few years and was no longer dependent on regular 9–5 work. I've done it! I've lived the life that so many people dream of, one in which I could pursue my passions and yet accumulate riches. The knowledge I'm about to impart to you in this book has been influenced by the experiences I've had along the way. *"The Passive Path to Prosperity"* is not only a book, it is a path to financial independence. I wrote this book with you in mind—for individuals who want to live a life free from financial restraints, where money serves as a tool rather than a barrier. I want you to see your potential as you peruse these pages. The tactics I provide here are not exclusive to the affluent or the extraordinarily fortunate; rather, they are available to everyone who is prepared to make the first move. The ideas in this book may assist you in reaching financial independence in three years or less, regardless of where you are in your journey or how you choose to modify your strategy. You are free to travel this path, and I will be at your side every step of the way. Together, we'll examine the approaches that have benefited me and many others, as well as the attitude required to be successful in this undertaking. By the time you finish reading this book, you'll be equipped with the information and self-assurance necessary to start along your road to riches. Are you prepared to go on your trip now? Let's travel the journey together to financial independence that is waiting for us.

1

Understanding Passive Income

To begin, let's ask a question that is not only straightforward but also profound: what precisely is passive income? There is a lot of talk about the word these days, and it is often associated with pictures of people relaxing on the beach while their bank accounts are easily filled up. So, what exactly does it imply?

Money that you generate with little to no continuous work is referred to as passive income. Passive income, on the other hand, enables you to decouple your profits from the number of hours you work, in contrast to active income, which compels you to exchange your time for money **(think of your usual employment that runs**

from 9 to 5). This indicates that once your revenue is established, it will continue to pour in regardless of whether or not you are actively participating in the process from the beginning.

My quest for financial freedom begins with this essential insight. The conventional method of putting in long hours of labor for several years to save savings for retirement was not the only option available to me. There was another way—one where I could create cash even while I wasn't actively working. The notion of passive income opened up a world of possibilities, and I understood that this was the key to gaining the financial independence I sought.

But let's be clear: passive income is not a get-rich-quick plan. It needs early work, preparation, and often a considerable upfront expenditure, whether that's time, money, or both. On the other hand, the benefits are enormous. Imagine waking up every morning knowing that your financial stability is no longer bound to the hours you labor. That's the power of passive income.

Types of Passive Income Streams

Now that we understand what passive income is, let's delve into the numerous sorts of passive income sources. There's no one-size-fits-all method, and the beauty of passive income is that it can be adapted to your hobbies, abilities, and financial condition. Here are some of the most prevalent types:

Real Estate Investments

This is where my adventure started. Real estate is one of the most dependable and established methods to produce passive income. Whether it's rental properties, REITs (Real Estate Investment Trusts), or crowdfunding platforms, real estate provides a range of options to produce money passively. My first step into this was with a tiny duplex, which became the cornerstone of my financial freedom. The rental revenue from that home not only paid the mortgage but also generated a regular stream of cash flow that enabled me to invest in more properties.

Dividend Stocks

Investing in dividend-paying companies is another excellent strategy to produce passive income. Companies give a part of their income to shareholders in the form of dividends. By constructing a portfolio of dividend stocks, you may develop a regular income stream that rises over time as you reinvest the dividends. One of the primary advantages of this method is that it involves very little continuing effort—once you've picked your stocks, you can sit back and watch your dividends stream in.

Digital Products and Online Businesses

In today's digital era, developing and selling digital products—such as eBooks, online courses, or software—can be a potentially profitable kind of passive income. Once your product is built and released, it may continue to generate sales and money for years to come with no upkeep. My experience as an independent author on Amazon KDP has taught me directly how digital items can become a stable source of passive income. The initial labor of creating and publishing a book pays off as it continues to sell long after the writing is done, the same can be applied to any field of skill you have, which can be monetized and then turned to passive income.

Peer-to-Peer Lending

Peer-to-peer lending systems enable you to lend money directly to people or small companies in return for interest payments. This may be a fantastic strategy to produce passive income, but it's vital to recognize the dangers involved. While the rewards might be appealing, there's always the danger that the borrower can fail on the loan. It's a higher-risk, higher-reward alternative, but with proper selection, it may be a significant element of your passive income portfolio.

Royalties

Royalties are payments you earn for the continued use of your intellectual property, such as a book, music, or patent. As I said previously, my books on Amazon KDP earn royalties each time a copy is sold. This is a real sort of passive income—once the work is generated, the royalties continue to trickle in without any additional effort on your side. It's a terrific method to monetize your ideas and knowledge over the long run.

These are just a few examples of passive income sources, but the possibilities are unlimited. The goal is to uncover what resonates with you and matches your abilities and resources. Don't be scared to experiment and explore alternative options. Remember, the idea is to develop many sources of income that work together to improve your financial stability.

Myths and Realities of Passive Income

Now, let's address some of the frequent fallacies and misunderstandings concerning passive income. It's easy to get caught up in the hoopla, but it's crucial to approach this issue with a clear and practical perspective.

Myth 1

Passive Income is Easy Money

One of the greatest illusions regarding passive income is that it's simple money—just put it up and watch the bucks stream in. The fact is that building passive income streams needs work, especially at the outset. Whether you're purchasing rental properties, trading in stocks, or producing digital businesses, there's an initial learning curve and a large amount of labor required. However, once the processes are in place, the income may certainly become more hands-off. But make no mistake, passive income is far from straightforward.

Myth 2
You Need a Lot of Money to Start

Another prevalent myth is that you need a substantial amount of cash to start producing passive income. While having money to invest will undoubtedly speed your growth, it's not a need. Many passive income sources, such as developing digital items or running a blog, require little to no initial commitment. My adventure began with a modest investment in a tiny duplex, and from there, I reinvested my profits to increase my portfolio. The trick is to start with what you have and grow from there.

Myth 3
Passive Income is Risk-Free

No investment or income source is fully risk-free, and passive income is no exception. Real estate markets may vary, renters can be unreliable, and stock values might decline. However, knowing and managing these risks is part of the process. Diversification is one of the greatest methods to limit risk—by spreading your investments over numerous assets and income sources, you decrease the effect of any one failure. The idea isn't to eliminate risk but to manage it efficiently.

Reality Of Passive Income

Passive Income Can Change Your Life
Despite these beliefs, the fact is that passive income can revolutionize your financial life. It allows the freedom and flexibility to live on your terms, free from the restraints of a regular career. My own life has been revolutionized by the passive income streams I've developed, enabling me to follow my hobbies, spend time with loved ones, and live with a feeling of financial security. It's not a short or simple journey, but it's worth every ounce of work.

The Mindset Shift
From Active to Passive

One of the most crucial components of moving to passive income is the mentality change from active to passive. This transformation is not only about altering how you make money; it's about changing how you think about money, time, and work. In the old approach, we're conditioned to assume that hard effort is directly proportional to achievement. The more hours we put in, the more we earn. But with passive income, success is determined not by how hard you work, but by how clever you work.

It's about using your time and resources to develop systems that produce cash without your continual engagement.

This mentality adjustment might be tough, particularly if you've spent your whole life working in a typical job. It needs you to think differently about how you value your time and to accept the concept that your money may work harder for you than you can for it. For me, this transformation was gradual. It wasn't easy to let go of the comfort of a regular income and embrace the volatility of business and investment. But once I plunged, I never looked back.

To succeed on this trip, you need to take a long-term view. Passive income is not about instant gratification—it's about creating a foundation for financial independence that will benefit you for years to come. This demands patience, tenacity, and a willingness to take measured risks. But most importantly, it involves conviction in yourself and the process.

I want to underline that this path is not only about money—it's about recovering your time, your energy, and your life.

Passive income is the instrument that enables you to live on your terms, follow your hobbies, and spend your time doing what matters to you. It's a route to freedom, and the first step is altering the way you think about money and wealth.

2

Leveraging Inflation

Your Secret Weapon

Inflation is one of those financial concepts that everyone speaks about but few comprehend. Inflation is the pace at which the overall level of prices for goods and services grows, diminishing the buying power of your money. In other words, the $100 you have now won't purchase as much in ten years as it does now. This may seem like awful news, and for many, it is. But for those of us who know how to use it, inflation may be a strong friend on the path to financial freedom. I learned about inflation the hard way. Early in my work, I was dutifully accumulating money in a low-interest savings account, believing that I was doing everything properly. But as the years passed, I realized something unsettling—my funds weren't rising quite as rapidly as I'd imagined.

THE PASSIVE PATH TO PROSPERITY

When I factored in inflation, I realized I was losing buying power. It was a wake-up call that made me reassess my whole approach to generating money.

Inflation isn't something to be dreaded; it's a fact of the economic world we live in. The key is to understand how it affects your financial condition and how you may utilize it to your advantage. For many individuals, inflation erodes their savings, but for those who know how to invest intelligently, inflation may help enhance their wealth. The answer is in identifying assets that not only maintain pace with inflation but surpass it.

Let me offer a personal story: In my early days of investing, I once bought a brand-new automobile, convinced that I was making a great financial decision. It was flashy, trustworthy, and seemed like a prize for my hard work. However, after only a few years, I saw that the expense of maintaining it, along with the diminishing value of the automobile itself, made it less of an asset and more of a problem. Meanwhile, inflation has slowly raised the price of equivalent new automobiles. Had I placed that money in a home or a stock portfolio instead, I would have likely experienced a rise in value rather than a drop. This incident taught me a crucial lesson: Not all spending is created equal, and in an inflationary atmosphere, where you put your money matters more than ever. Understanding inflation's influence on various kinds of assets is vital for making educated financial choices. Some assets lose value when inflation increases, while others, like real estate and some equities, might gain value.

In this chapter, we're going to discuss how you might transform inflation into an opportunity rather than a danger. By knowing how inflation works and how it impacts various kinds of assets, you'll be better positioned to safeguard your money and potentially exploit inflation to hasten your road toward financial independence.

Turning Inflation into Opportunity

Once I comprehended the notion of inflation and its ability to erode the value of my money, I started to view it in a different light—as a tool that might operate for me rather than against me. **But how can you convert something as apparently negative as inflation into an opportunity?** <u>The solution lies in leveraging debt and assets that grow over time.</u> Let's take real estate, for example. When you purchase a house with a mortgage, you're effectively borrowing money at today's value, but you'll be paying it back with tomorrow's depreciated dollars. If inflation increases, the value of the property normally rises, but your mortgage payments stay the same. This implies that when inflation drives the value of your property higher, your debt essentially gets cheaper in real terms.

I recall when I acquired my first rental property. At the time, interest rates were quite low, and I locked in a fixed-rate mortgage. Over the years, as inflation pushed up the cost of living, rentals grew, but my mortgage payments kept the same. This disparity between my fixed expenditures and growing rental revenue became a substantial source of profit, enabling me to reinvest and expand my portfolio even more. But real estate isn't the only option to transform inflation into an opportunity. Investments in commodities, like gold or oil, generally increase with inflation, making them an excellent hedge against increasing costs. Stocks, particularly those in corporations with great pricing power, may also gain as these businesses pass on increased prices to customers, preserving or even growing their profit margins.

The goal is to concentrate on assets that increase over time and to avoid investments that are likely to lose value when inflation rises.

Cash, for example, is one of the worst places to be during times of rising inflation since its purchase value is constantly destroyed.

By understanding this dynamic, you can make educated choices that safeguard and build your wealth, even when inflation rises.

Inflation-Proof Investments

So, what are some inflation-proof assets that might help you not just survive but prosper in an inflationary environment? The solution to this issue depends on knowing which assets tend to do well while prices are increasing.

Real Estate

As we covered before, real estate is one of the finest inflation-proof assets. Properties often rise in value with time, particularly during times of strong inflation. This is because real estate is a physical asset that frequently gets more valuable when the cost of materials and labor rises. Additionally, rental revenue frequently stays pace with or surpasses inflation, giving a consistent source of cash flow that rises in real terms.

Stocks

Equities, especially those in firms that may pass on increased prices to customers, are another effective hedge against inflation. Look for firms with strong brands, necessary goods, or services that consumers will continue to purchase despite price rises. These enterprises frequently have the pricing power to retain profitability, even in an inflationary market. Dividend-paying stocks may also offer a stream of income that tends to rise over time, helping you stay pace with inflation.

Commodities

Investing in commodities like gold, silver, or oil may also be a sensible decision during inflationary situations. These assets often grow in value when the cost of goods and services rises, making them a suitable hedge against inflation. I recall diversifying my portfolio with some gold assets during a moment of economic instability. While I didn't see immediate returns, the value of my investment climbed slowly as inflation took hold, offering a good cushion against the loss of my spending power.

Inflation-Protected Bonds

For individuals who want a more cautious strategy, inflation-protected bonds, such as Treasury Inflation-Protected Securities (TIPS), might be a viable alternative. These bonds are intended to rise in value with inflation, ensuring that your investment maintains pace with increasing costs. While they may not provide the high returns of stocks or real estate, they give a solid means to preserve your principal and make a small return in an inflationary economy.

Diversifying your investments among five inflation-proof assets will help you develop a robust portfolio that not only withstands the ravages of inflation but also capitalizes on the possibilities it brings. The goal is to be educated, be proactive, and make changes as required to guarantee that your wealth continues to increase, no matter what the economic condition.

Adapting Strategies in an Inflationary Economy

Inflation isn't a static force—it varies over time, and your investing plan should adjust appropriately. Understanding how to change your strategy as the economic climate develops is vital to keeping and expanding your wealth. When I initially began investing, I made the error of believing that my original method would always be successful. But when inflation varied, I soon understood that what worked in a low-inflation scenario didn't always hold up when inflation rates started to climb. This showed me the necessity of being adaptable and being prepared to modify my plan in response to changing situations.

One method to adapt is by frequently examining your investment portfolio and rebalancing it to ensure that it stays aligned with your financial objectives and the current economic situation. For example, during times of increasing inflation, you could wish to increase your exposure to assets like real estate, commodities, or inflation-protected bonds, **while lowering your holdings in cash or fixed-income instruments that are more exposed to inflation.**

Another crucial part of adjusting your plan is remaining updated about economic trends and statistics. Keep a watch on inflation rates, interest rates, and other crucial measures that might affect your assets. By remaining informed, you may anticipate changes and make adjustments before they have a big influence on your portfolio.

Finally, don't be scared to seek out new chances that occur in an inflationary environment. As prices increase, some sectors and businesses may offer unique investing possibilities. For example, organizations that provide critical products and services, or those that profit from increased commodity prices, may offer favorable returns during inflationary times. Be open to examining these possibilities and altering your plan to capitalize on them.
In conclusion, leveraging inflation to your benefit involves a mix of knowledge, strategy, and flexibility. By

taking the time to grasp how inflation affects your assets and by keeping flexible in your strategy, you can transform this economic force into a strong weapon on your journey to financial independence. **Remember, inflation doesn't have to be your enemy—it may be your hidden weapon.**

3

Setting Financial Goals for Independence

The route to financial freedom starts with a clear objective in mind—your **Financial Freedom Number.** This figure shows the amount of money you need to have invested or saved to meet your living needs eternally, without having to work for a wage. For many, this figure represents the ultimate objective, the point at which they may live life on their terms.

When I initially began my journey to financial freedom, I had no clue what my Financial Freedom Number was. I knew I wanted to escape the daily grind, but without a defined aim, my efforts seemed dispersed. It wasn't until

I sat down and estimated precisely how much I needed to pay my expenses—both necessary and discretionary—that my trip got focused. To establish your Financial Freedom Number, start by taking an honest look at your present costs. Break them down into categories: housing, food, transportation, entertainment, travel, and any other areas that are essential to you. Then, consider how these costs could alter after you're financially independent. Will you travel more? Spend more on hobbies? Or possibly downsize your living situation?

Once you have a thorough grasp of your costs, the next step is to establish how much you need to invest to earn that amount of money passively.

A classic rule of thumb is the 4% rule, which implies that you may safely remove 4% of your investment portfolio each year without exhausting your capital. For example, if your yearly costs are $50,000, your Financial Freedom Number would be $1.25 million ($50,000 divided by 0.04). Defining your Financial Freedom

Number offers you a realistic target to aim toward. It also gives clarity and incentive, translating the abstract notion of financial independence into a specific, reachable milestone. Remember, the path may be lengthy, but with a clear destination in sight, every step takes you closer to ultimate financial independence.

Short-Term vs. Long-Term Goals

As you strive toward financial independence, it's vital to establish both short-term and long-term objectives. Short-term objectives give fast gains and keep you motivated, while long-term goals keep you focused on the greater picture. When I initially began investing in real estate, my long-term aim was to establish a portfolio of rental properties that would provide enough passive income to pay my living costs. But that aim seemed difficult, perhaps overpowering. To keep motivated, I divided it down into smaller, more realistic short-term goals: **save for the down payment on my first property, refurbish it to boost its worth, and then locate dependable renters.** Each of these short-term objectives was a step toward my greater vision, and attaining them created a feeling of achievement that kept me going ahead. Over time, these modest successes built up, and before I realized it, I had accomplished my long-term objective of financial independence.

When defining your objectives, it's crucial to create a balance between the two. Your long-term objectives should be ambitious and inspiring—something that stimulates you and makes you want to press ahead, even when the going gets rough. Your short-term objectives, on the other hand, should be reasonable and reachable, allowing you frequent occasions to celebrate your achievement. For example, a long-term goal may be to save $500,000 in the next 10 years, while a short-term goal might be to save $10,000 in the next six months. By breaking down your long-term objectives into smaller stages, you make the route to financial freedom more doable and enjoyable. In the end, both short-term and long-term objectives are crucial for success. The short-term objectives keep you motivated and on track, while the long-term goals guarantee that your efforts are driving you to your ultimate destination—financial independence.

Tracking Progress and Adjusting Plans

Setting objectives is merely the first step; measuring your success and changing your plans as required is where the real work starts. Financial freedom is not a straight path—it's riddled with twists, turns, and unforeseen diversions. By periodically monitoring your progress and being open to change, you can traverse these hurdles and remain on track. Early in my trip, I made the error of defining my objectives and then putting them on autopilot, believing that everything would go according to plan. But life doesn't operate that way. The real estate market changed, unanticipated bills popped up, and certain assets didn't perform as well as I had intended. At first, these failures were disappointing, but I soon recognized that they were part of the process. One of the most essential things I learned was the importance of flexibility. When things didn't go as planned, I learned to pivot—whether that meant altering my savings rate, investigating other investment options, or even reassessing my long-term objectives. By being flexible and keeping a careful watch on my progress, I was able to transform possible obstacles into chances for improvement.

To monitor your progress, try setting up frequent check-ins—whether monthly, quarterly, or annually—where you analyze your financial condition and determine whether you're on pace to accomplish your objectives.

Are your assets functioning as expected? Do your expenses match your spending plan? Do you need to modify your savings rate or seek other income streams? If you realize that you're lagging, don't be dismayed. Use it as a chance to learn and make corrections. The route to financial freedom is a marathon, not a sprint, and it's the capacity to adapt that will eventually lead to success. Remember, development isn't always linear. There may be ups and downs, but by monitoring your progress and revising your goals as required, you'll guarantee that you remain on the road to financial independence.

Celebrating Milestones Along the Way

Financial independence is a long-term objective that demands patience, discipline, and endurance. But it doesn't imply you should wait until you reach your ultimate destination to rejoice. Celebrating milestones along the road is vital for retaining motivation and keeping involved in the process. When I reached my first significant milestone—paying off the mortgage on my first rental property—I celebrated with a minor victory: a weekend vacation with my family. It wasn't lavish, but it was a meaningful gesture to appreciate the hard work and dedication that had brought me to that place. This celebration renewed my desire and reminded me of why

I had gone on this road in the first place.Celebrating milestones doesn't have to be expensive or complex. It might be as easy as rewarding yourself with a good meal, taking a day off to unwind, or simply just sharing your achievement with loved ones. The idea is to acknowledge the progress you've made and use it as fuel to keep going.Some milestones you can consider celebrating include attaining a particular savings target, making your first profitable investment, paying off a large debt, or earning a certain amount of passive income. Each of these milestones is a step closer to financial freedom, and appreciating them helps reinforce the attitudes and behaviors that will lead to long-term success. Celebrating milestones also gives you a chance to reflect on your path. What techniques have worked well? What difficulties have you overcome? How have you evolved along the way? By taking the time to celebrate and reflect, you'll develop a greater appreciation for the process and a revitalized sense of purpose as you continue on your journey. In the end, the road to financial freedom is as vital as the goal. By establishing clear objectives, charting your progress, and celebrating your accomplishments, you'll not only attain financial independence but also build a life full of purpose, development, and pleasure.

4

Budgeting for Success

Budgeting is the cornerstone of financial success. It's not just about monitoring costs; it's about taking control of your financial destiny. A well-crafted budget helps you to use your resources efficiently, ensuring that you live within your means while working towards your financial objectives. When I first started budgeting, I was **intimidated** by the concept of recording every cost. My original approach was to develop a sophisticated spreadsheet that rapidly became more of a hassle than useful. I struggled to stay with it, and my money management seemed like a never-ending fight. It wasn't until I streamlined my budgeting technique that I began seeing significant improvements.

Here's what worked for me: I started by documenting my income and fixed expenses—things like rent, utilities, and insurance. Next, I developed categories for variable spending, such as grocery, entertainment, and eating out. Instead of concentrating on minute details, I established broad spending limitations for each area and made sure to adapt as required. One key to good budgeting is making it a habit. Set up a dedicated period each week to examine your expenditures and change your budget as required. You don't have to do it alone—consider utilizing budgeting applications that can automatically monitor your expenditure and give insights into your financial patterns.

Another crucial component of budgeting is creating financial objectives. Whether you're saving for a trip, paying off debt, or investing for the future, dedicate a percentage of your budget to these objectives. Seeing your progress towards these objectives will keep you motivated and focused. Remember, budgeting isn't about limiting yourself; it's about making educated decisions that match your financial objectives. By designing a budget that works for you and adhering to it, you'll create a strong foundation for reaching financial freedom.

Eliminating Debt Efficiently

Debt may be a huge hurdle on the path to financial freedom. High-interest debt, in particular, may destroy your wealth and inhibit your advancement. Eliminating debt effectively is vital for freeing up resources to invest and grow wealth. When I began battling my debt, I felt intimidated by the overall amount I owed. I had credit card debt, college debts, and a vehicle loan, and it looked like an enormous problem. I realized I needed a plan, so I studied several techniques and finally found success with the debt snowball method.

Here's how it works: List all your debts from lowest to highest. Focus on paying off the lowest debt first while making minimum payments on the rest. Once the lowest debt is paid off, go on to the next one. This strategy develops momentum and offers a psychological lift as you watch debts vanishing.

Another technique to explore is the debt avalanche method, where you prioritize paying off loans with the highest interest rates first. This technique may save you more money in interest over time, but it may take longer to see specific loans vanish. Regardless of the strategy you use, the important is to be disciplined and devoted. Cut down on needless costs, improve your income if feasible, and put any additional money toward your debt. Celebrate each milestone—paying off a debt is a huge accomplishment and should be honored. Remember, removing debt is not only about freeing up money; it's about restoring control over your financial life. By handling debt effectively, you'll be better positioned to invest, save, and accomplish your financial objectives.

Creating an Emergency Fund

An emergency fund is your financial safety net, meant to cover unforeseen bills and offer peace of mind.

It's an essential component of a good financial foundation and may prevent you from derailing your financial progress when life throws you a curveball. I recall when I suffered a surprise job loss some years ago. Without an emergency fund, I was forced to delve into my savings and take on additional debt to support my living needs. It was a difficult moment, and I learned firsthand the value of having a financial buffer. To establish your emergency fund, start by choosing a goal amount. A usual guideline is to save three to six months' worth of living costs. This investment should be immediately accessible, so consider placing it in a high-yield savings account or a money market account. Start small if necessary—saving even a tiny amount each month may build up over time. Automate your savings by setting up a direct payment into your emergency fund, so you're continually growing your buffer without having to worry about it. **Avoid utilizing your emergency money for non-emergencies.** It's tempting to delve into it for scheduled spending or lifestyle changes but remember, its role is to offer a safety net for unexpected crises. By keeping your emergency fund intact, you'll be better prepared to face unexpected shocks without endangering your long-term objectives.Creating an emergency fund is not only about financial readiness; it's about allowing yourself to confront unforeseen circumstances with confidence. With a healthy emergency fund in place, you'll be able to negotiate life's difficulties without derailing your road to financial freedom.

The Importance of Financial Literacy

Financial literacy is the basis of good money management. It's about knowing how money works, making educated choices, and developing the skills to attain financial objectives. Without financial knowledge, even the finest financial strategies may fall short. Early in my financial path, I discovered that my lack of understanding was holding me back. I grasped the fundamentals of saving and investing, but I struggled with more sophisticated topics like asset allocation, tax strategies, and retirement planning. I realized I needed to educate myself to make educated judgments. *One of the greatest ways to enhance your financial literacy is to read books, attend classes, and seek guidance from financial professionals.* I discovered that investing in my education paid me rewards, enabling me to make wiser financial decisions and prevent expensive blunders. In addition to formal instruction, interact with personal financial networks and forums. Discussing financial plans with others may bring helpful insights and diverse viewpoints. Don't be hesitant to ask questions or seek assistance when needed—financial literacy is a lifetime process, and ongoing learning is vital. Another crucial part of financial literacy is knowing your financial habits. Reflect on your spending patterns, saving preferences, and investing methods. Identifying areas where you may improve can help you design a more successful financial strategy. By emphasizing financial literacy, you empower yourself to make educated choices and take charge of your financial destiny. Investing in your knowledge is one of the finest strategies to develop a strong financial foundation and attain long-term success.

5

EXPLORING INVESTMENT OPPORTUNITIES

Stock Market Basics

The stock market is often the first stop for many people looking to invest and build wealth. Understanding the basics of stock market investing is crucial for making informed decisions and growing your financial portfolio. When I first dipped my toes into the stock market, I was both excited and intimidated. I remember investing in a few tech stocks I'd read about, driven more by enthusiasm than by a solid strategy. The result? A rollercoaster of gains and losses that taught me a lot about the importance of research and strategy. There is a location where you can purchase and sell shares of corporations, and that area is the stock market. Shares are a representation of ownership in a firm, and the value of those shares may change depending on the performance of the company as well as the circumstances of the market as a whole. The goal is to buy shares at a lower price and sell them at a higher price, thereby making a profit. One fundamental concept to understand is diversification: **spreading your investments across different sectors and companies to reduce risk. Instead of putting all your money into a single stock, consider investing in a mix of stocks across various industries. If one industry is not performing as expected, this might help offset losses.**

Another important aspect is understanding different types of stocks. Common stocks give you voting rights and potential dividends, while preferred stocks usually offer fixed dividends but no voting rights. Each type has its own risk and reward profile, so choose based on your investment goals and risk tolerance. Index funds and ETFs (Exchange-Traded Funds) are also great options for beginners. They're often less volatile than individual stocks and can provide steady growth over time. Understanding the stock market is fundamental to creating a successful investment strategy. It can seem complex at first, but breaking it down into manageable concepts makes it more accessible. Let's explore the basics of stock market investing, including how it works, key concepts, and practical tips to get started.

How the Stock Market Works

The stock market operates through various exchanges, such as the New York Stock Exchange (NYSE) and the Nasdaq. These exchanges provide a marketplace for buying and selling stocks, and they ensure that transactions are conducted fairly and transparently.

Key Concepts to Understand

Stock Prices and Market Orders

Stock prices fluctuate based on supply and demand. When more individuals desire to purchase a stock, the price of that stock goes up. On the other hand, if there are more individuals keen to sell, the price will decrease. Market orders are the most straightforward type of trade, where you buy or sell a stock at the current market price. Limit orders allow you to specify the price at which you want to buy or sell, offering more control over your trades.Early in my investing journey, I made the mistake of placing market orders without considering the impact of price fluctuations. I learned that using limit orders can help you manage costs and avoid buying or selling at unfavorable prices.

Bull and bear markets

A bull market is characterized by rising stock prices and investor confidence, while a bear market features declining prices and pessimism. Understanding these market trends helps you gauge overall market conditions and adjust your investment strategy accordingly. I experienced both bull and bear markets during my investing career. During a bull market, I focused on growth stocks and aggressive strategies. In a bear market, I shifted to more conservative investments and sought opportunities in undervalued stocks.

Dividends

Typically derived from a company's earnings, dividends are payments that are provided by businesses to their shareholders. They provide a consistent flow of income and may be re-invested in so that further shares can be purchased. Dividend-paying stocks are often favored by investors looking for regular income and stability. One of my favorite investments has been in dividend-paying stocks. The dividends provided a consistent income, which I reinvested to compound my returns. Companies with a strong history of dividend payments can offer stability and a reliable source of income.

Market Indices

Market indices, like the S&P 500 or Dow Jones Industrial Average, track the performance of a group of stocks and provide a snapshot of overall market health. Investing in index funds or ETFs that track these indices can offer broad market exposure and diversification. I initially focused on individual stocks but later realized the benefits of investing in index funds. They provided exposure to a wide range of companies, reducing my risk and offering consistent returns aligned with overall market performance.

Practical Tips for Beginners

Start with Research

Before investing, take the time to research companies, industries, and market trends. Look at financial statements, company performance, and industry news. Reliable sources, such as financial news websites and analyst reports, can provide valuable insights. My research approach evolved from relying on news headlines to conducting an in-depth analysis of company fundamentals and market conditions. This shift improved my investment decisions and helped me identify promising opportunities.

Diversify Your Portfolio

Diversification involves spreading your investments across different stocks, sectors, and asset classes. It helps reduce risk by ensuring that poor performance in one area doesn't drastically impact your overall portfolio. Early in my investing career, I concentrated too heavily on technology stocks. Diversifying into various sectors, such as healthcare, finance, and consumer goods, balanced my portfolio and mitigated the impact of market volatility.

Invest for the Long Term

The stock market can be volatile in the short term, but historically, it has shown positive growth over the long term. Develop a long-term investment strategy and avoid making impulsive decisions based on short-term market movements.I learned this lesson the hard way by reacting to market fluctuations and making hasty decisions. Committing to a long-term strategy allowed me to benefit from compounding returns and ride out market downturns.

Regularly Review and Rebalance

Review your investment portfolio on a regular basis to verify that it is in line with your financial objectives and the amount of risk you are willing to take. Rebalancing involves adjusting your portfolio to maintain your desired asset allocation and manage risk effectively.Rebalancing became a crucial part of my investment strategy. It ensured that my portfolio remained aligned with my goals and adapted to changes in market conditions and personal circumstances.

Common Mistakes to Avoid

Chasing Hot Tips

Avoid making investment decisions based solely on hot tips or trends. Thoroughly research and evaluate investments based on your financial goals and risk tolerance. I once chased a hot stock tip without proper research and ended up with a loss. Developing a disciplined approach to investing, based on research and strategy, proved more effective in the long run.

Timing the Market

Trying to time the market by predicting highs and lows is challenging and often leads to missed opportunities. Instead, focus on a consistent investment strategy and regular contributions to build wealth over time. I initially attempted to time the market but found that consistent investing and maintaining a long-term perspective yielded better results. Dollar-cost averaging, or investing a fixed amount regularly, helped smooth out the impact of market volatility.

Ignoring Fees

Be aware of fees associated with buying and selling stocks, as well as management fees for investment funds. Over time, high fees might reduce the amount of money you make. I learned to scrutinize fees and choose low-cost investment options. This practice helped maximize my returns and ensured that fees did not detract from my investment gains.

Conclusion

Understanding stock market basics is a crucial step in your investment journey. By grasping key concepts like stock prices, market orders, and diversification, and by applying practical tips and avoiding common mistakes, you can build a solid foundation for successful investing. The stock market offers vast growth opportunities, and with informed decision-making and a long-term perspective, you can harness its potential to achieve financial independence. Keep in mind that the stock market is not a plan to get wealthy overnight. It demands patience, investigation, and a long-term view. Start with a solid strategy, invest regularly, and keep learning as you go. With time and effort, you can build a strong portfolio that contributes significantly to your path to financial independence.

Real Estate Investments

Real estate investment may be a great strategy to develop wealth and earn passive income. Whether you're purchasing rental properties, flipping houses, or investing in real estate investment trusts (REITs), real estate offers numerous opportunities for financial growth. My journey into real estate began with a single-family rental property. Initially, I was nervous about the responsibilities of being a landlord and managing property. I spent countless hours researching locations, calculating potential returns, and learning about property management. It was a high learning curve, but the benefits were worth it. One important element to successful real estate investment is location.

Investing in properties in growing or desirable areas can lead to higher rental income and property appreciation.

Look for neighborhoods with good schools, low crime rates, and strong economic growth.

Also, consider the property's condition and potential for improvement.Rental properties can provide a steady stream of passive income, but they also come with responsibilities. Ensure you screen tenants carefully, maintain the property regularly, and budget for unexpected expenses, such as repairs or vacancies. If the idea of managing physical properties isn't appealing, consider investing in REITs. Because REITs are listed on large stock exchanges, investors may easily access and liquidate these assets. Diversification is also important in real estate. Instead of putting all your money into one property, consider investing in different types of real estate or various geographic locations to spread your risk. Real estate investing requires careful planning and management, but with the right approach, it can provide substantial returns and contribute significantly to your financial independence. Real estate is a time-tested avenue for building wealth and generating passive income. It offers unique opportunities that can complement other investment strategies and provide significant returns. Let's dive deeper into the various aspects of real estate investments, including different property types, strategies, and key considerations.

Types of Real Estate Investments

Residential Properties

These consist of vacation rentals, multi-family housing, and single-family dwellings. Investing in residential real estate often involves buying properties to rent out to tenants. It's a popular choice for many investors due to the potential for steady rental income and property appreciation. My first residential property was a modest single-family home in a growing suburb. I had to navigate tenant screening, property management, and maintenance. Initially, it was a learning curve, but over time, I understood the importance of choosing the right location and maintaining the property well. The steady rental income and property appreciation were rewarding and helped me build a solid foundation for further investments.

Commercial Properties

These include office buildings, retail spaces, and industrial properties. Commercial real estate often provides higher rental yields compared to residential properties, but it also comes with its own set of challenges, such as longer vacancy periods and higher maintenance costs. One of my ventures into commercial real estate involved purchasing a small retail building. It required a different approach, from negotiating longer-term leases with businesses to managing large-scale renovations. While the process was more complex, the higher rental income and the stability of long-term leases made it worthwhile.

Real Estate Investment Trusts (REITs)

Companies that own, manage, or finance real estate that generates income are known as REITs. They offer a way to invest in real estate without directly owning property. REITs are traded on major stock exchanges and can provide dividends and capital appreciation. I began investing in REITs to diversify my portfolio and gain exposure to different types of real estate without hands-on management. They offered liquidity and the ability to invest in high-quality properties across various sectors, from residential to commercial real estate.

Investment Strategies

Buy-and-Hold

This strategy involves purchasing properties and holding them for the long term. The intention is to profit from both property appreciation and rental revenue. This approach requires patience and a long-term perspective but can provide substantial rewards over time. My buy-and-hold strategy involved acquiring rental properties in emerging neighborhoods. By holding onto these properties, I was able to benefit from both rental income and significant property value increases as the areas developed.

Fix-and-Flip

This approach entails purchasing properties at a discount, making necessary renovations, and then reselling them for a profit. It can offer quick returns but requires a keen eye for potential, an understanding of renovation costs, and a solid plan for marketing the property.I had a few fix-and-flip projects early in my investment career. While the potential for high returns was appealing, the process involved managing renovation budgets, timelines, and market conditions. It was a high-stakes approach that required careful planning and execution.

Real Estate Crowdfunding

This method allows investors to pool their money to invest in larger real estate projects or developments. It provides access to real estate opportunities that might be otherwise out of reach for individual investors.I participated in a few real estate crowdfunding ventures to diversify my investment and explore different types of properties. It provided exposure to larger projects and allowed me to invest in real estate developments without the need for significant capital.

Key Considerations

Location

A property's potential for rental income and value may be greatly impacted by its location. Research the local real estate market, consider economic factors, and look for areas with growth potential. When selecting properties, I always considered the neighborhood's future outlook, proximity to amenities, and local market trends. Investing in areas with strong economic indicators and infrastructure development proved beneficial.

Financing

Understand the various financing options available for real estate investments, such as traditional mortgages, hard money loans, and private financing. Choose the option that aligns with your investment strategy and financial situation. My experience with financing involved exploring different loan options and understanding their implications on cash flow and returns. I found that securing favorable financing terms was crucial for maximizing profitability.

Property Management

Sustaining the worth of your investment and guaranteeing tenant contentment need efficient property management. Choose whether you want to employ a property management firm or manage the property yourself.

Peer-to-Peer Lending

Peer-to-peer (P2P) lending is a relatively new investment avenue that allows individuals to lend money directly to other individuals or businesses through online platforms. It's an innovative way to earn interest on your money while helping borrowers access funds they might not get through traditional financial institutions.My first foray into P2P lending was through a popular online platform that offered a range of lending opportunities. I was intrigued by the potential for high returns but also cautious about the risks involved. My initial experience taught me the importance of research and diversification in this investment space. P2P lending platforms connect lenders with borrowers, often providing higher interest rates than traditional savings accounts or bonds. However, it's crucial to understand that these loans come with varying levels of risk. Borrowers may have different credit profiles, and the likelihood of default can vary significantly.To mitigate risk, diversify your investments across multiple loans and borrowers. Many platforms allow you to spread your investment across many loans, reducing the impact of a single default on your overall portfolio. Additionally, thoroughly review borrower profiles and platform ratings to make informed decisions. One important consideration is the platform's track record and fees. Research the platform's history, user reviews, and fee structures before investing. Some platforms offer secondary markets where you can sell your loans if needed, providing liquidity in case you need to access your funds.P2P lending can offer attractive returns and a way to support individuals and small businesses. However, it requires careful management and understanding of the associated risks. By diversifying your investments and conducting thorough research, you can potentially benefit from this innovative investment opportunity.

How Peer-to-Peer Lending Works

Platforms for peer-to-peer lending serve as middlemen between investors and borrowers. Borrowers submit loan applications detailing their financial needs and creditworthiness, while investors review these applications and choose which loans to fund. The platform facilitates the transaction, manages repayments, and charges fees for its services.

Application and Approval

Borrowers apply for loans through P2P lending platforms by providing personal or business information and credit history. The platform evaluates the application, assigns a risk rating, and determines the interest rate based on the borrower's credit profile.

Investment and Funding

Investors browse available loan listings and select projects or individuals to fund based on their risk tolerance and desired return. Investments can be diversified across multiple loans to spread risk. Once a loan is fully funded, the borrower receives the funds, and investors begin receiving monthly interest payments. I initially started by funding small amounts across several loans to diversify my risk. This strategy helped me balance potential returns with the risk of borrower default.

Repayment and Returns

Borrowers make regular repayments, including principal and interest, over the loan term. Investors receive their share of these repayments according to the terms agreed upon. Platforms usually provide tools to track loan performance and manage investments. Tracking repayments and monitoring loan performance became a routine part of my investment strategy. Many platforms offer dashboards with detailed information about each loan, which helps in managing investments effectively.

Benefits of Peer-to-Peer Lending

Attractive Returns

Peer-to-peer lending can offer higher returns compared to traditional savings accounts or bonds. Interest rates on loans are often higher than those offered by banks, providing investors with an opportunity for better yields. I found P2P lending to be a valuable addition to my portfolio for generating higher returns.However, it's essential to understand the risk-return tradeoff and choose investments wisely.

Diversification

Investing in peer-to-peer loans allows for diversification beyond traditional asset classes like stocks and real estate. By spreading investments across different loans, sectors, and borrowers, you can reduce overall portfolio risk. Diversification was key in managing risk within my P2P lending investments. I allocated funds across various loans with different risk ratings and purposes to minimize the impact of any single borrower's default.

Social Impact
Peer-to-peer lending can also have a positive social impact by providing financing to individuals and small businesses that may not qualify for traditional bank loans. This can foster entrepreneurship and support community development.Supporting small businesses and individuals through P2P lending gave me a sense of contributing to economic growth. I chose to fund projects that aligned with my values and had the potential to make a positive difference.

Risks and Considerations
Credit Risk
One of the primary risks in P2P lending is borrower default. Unlike traditional bank loans, P2P lending

doesn't have government-backed insurance, so investors bear the risk of losing their principal if a borrower fails to repay. To mitigate credit risk, I thoroughly reviewed borrower profiles and chose loans with higher credit ratings and solid financial histories. Diversifying investments across multiple loans also helped manage this risk.

Platform Risk

The stability and reliability of the P2P lending platform itself is another factor to consider. If the platform encounters financial difficulties or operational issues, it could affect the management of your investments. I researched the credibility and financial health of the platforms I used, checking their track record, user reviews, and regulatory compliance. Choosing well-established platforms with strong reputations helped mitigate this risk.

Liquidity Risk

Unlike stocks or bonds, P2P loans are not easily tradable, which means your money is tied up for the duration of the loan term. This lack of liquidity can be a drawback if you need access to your funds before the loan matures. To address liquidity concerns, I maintained a portion of my portfolio in more liquid investments and used P2P lending as a complement rather than the primary investment vehicle.

Getting Started with Peer-to-Peer Lending

Choose a Platform

Select a reputable P2P lending platform that fits your investment goals and risk tolerance. Compare platforms based on their fee structures, loan offerings, and borrower vetting processes. I explored several platforms before committing. I looked for those with transparent fee structures, a wide range of loan options, and robust borrower screening processes.

Evaluate Loans

Carefully review loan listings and borrower profiles before investing. Consider factors such as credit ratings, loan purpose, interest rates, and repayment terms.

In my experience, performing due diligence on each loan helped me avoid high-risk investments and select opportunities with strong potential for returns.

Monitor and Adjust

Regularly monitor the performance of your P2P investments and make adjustments as needed. Stay informed about changes in platform policies, borrower performance, and market conditions. Regular monitoring and adjustment of my P2P lending portfolio allowed me to stay on top of performance and make informed decisions to optimize returns.

Conclusion

Peer-to-peer lending offers a distinctive approach to investing that can provide attractive returns and diversify your portfolio. By understanding how P2P lending works, recognizing its benefits and risks, and implementing a strategic approach, you can harness this investment opportunity to enhance your financial independence. Embrace the potential of P2P lending, and it may become a valuable component of your journey toward financial prosperity.

Diversifying Your Portfolio

Diversification is a critical strategy for managing risk and achieving financial growth. By spreading your investments across different asset classes, industries, and geographic regions, you can reduce the impact of poor performance in any single area of your portfolio. When I first began investing, I focused heavily on a single asset class: stocks. While this approach offered significant growth potential, it also exposed me to higher volatility. It wasn't until I diversified my investments that I experienced more stable returns and reduced risk. A diversified portfolio typically includes a mix of stocks, bonds, real estate, and other asset classes. Each asset class responds differently to market conditions, so combining them can help smooth out your returns. For example, stocks might perform well during economic expansions, while bonds can provide stability during downturns. Consider diversifying within asset classes as well.

For stocks, invest in different sectors, such as technology, healthcare, and consumer goods. For bonds, look at government, municipal, and corporate bonds. Real estate investments can also be diversified across residential, commercial, and industrial properties. Geographic diversification is another important aspect. Investing in international markets can provide exposure to growth opportunities outside your home country and reduce the impact of domestic economic fluctuations. Make sure your portfolio is in line with your financial objectives and risk tolerance by reviewing and adjusting it on a regular basis. Rebalancing is modifying your portfolio to preserve the asset allocation you have chosen. Over time, certain assets may grow faster than others, skewing your portfolio's balance. Rebalancing helps keep your portfolio aligned with your long-term strategy. Diversification doesn't guarantee profits or protect against losses, but it's a powerful tool for managing risk and achieving steady growth. By building a well-diversified portfolio, you'll be better positioned to weather market fluctuations and stay on track toward financial independence.

6

CREATING MULTIPLE INCOME STREAMS

Achieving financial independence isn't only about decreasing expenditures and saving; it's also about boosting your income. One of the most efficient ways to achieve this is by generating various revenue sources. Building several revenue sources is a cornerstone of financial freedom. It not only offers financial stability but also speeds your road toward riches by harnessing multiple income streams. In this chapter, we'll discuss how to discover possible revenue sources, balance active and passive income, grow your income streams, and automate them so your money works for you, not the other way around.

Identifying Potential Income Sources

The first step in developing several revenue streams is identifying the possible possibilities around you. Income streams may be classed generally into earned income (active) and unearned income (passive). To discover the correct sources, start by examining your skills, interests, and resources.

Exploring Earned Income

Earned income is what you get in return for your time and work. This may involve day employment, freelancing, consulting, or even part-time work. If you have particular abilities, try providing them on services like Upwork or Fiverr. For example, if you're good at graphic design, web development, or writing, you may monetize these abilities in your free time. In my quest, I learned I had an aptitude for teaching and started delivering online classes. It began as a side venture but turned into a considerable cash source. The idea is to look at what you're already strong at and discover methods to monetize those abilities.

Tapping into Passive Income

Passive income is money produced with minimum effort after the initial setup. It might come from investments, rental properties, royalties from creative work, or dividends from stocks. To find passive income prospects, assess what assets you currently have or can obtain. For instance, if you own property, renting it out might create a stable income. If you're interested in the stock market, dividend-paying companies might be a smart alternative. When I initially invested in real estate, it was a struggle to handle everything actively. However, over time, I automated the procedures and made them into a passive revenue stream, enabling me to concentrate on other businesses.

Balancing Active and Passive Income

A well-rounded financial plan comprises a mix of active and passive revenue sources. Active income offers you instant cash flow, which may be reinvested into passive income prospects. Over time, the idea is to move the balance towards passive income, ensuring financial security without ongoing work.

Finding the Right Balance

The balance between active and passive income relies on your present financial condition and long-term aspirations. In the beginning, your emphasis could be on developing active revenue sources to sustain oneself. As your financial buffer improves, you may start investing in passive income sources. For example, early in my career, I depended primarily on active revenue from my work and side hustles. But I always reinvested a part of that revenue into real estate and equities. As those assets developed, my passive income started to eclipse my active income, enabling me greater flexibility to select how I spent my time.

Avoiding Burnout

Managing many active revenue sources may lead to burnout if not managed appropriately. It's crucial to prioritize chores and automate when feasible. For instance, if you're starting a side company, consider outsourcing chores like bookkeeping or customer support, so you can concentrate on growth.I recall a point when I was juggling too many active tasks at once. It harmed both my productivity and health. By delegating responsibilities and concentrating on expanding passive income, I was able to strike a lasting balance that didn't compromise my well-being.

Scaling Your Income Streams

Once you have various revenue sources, the next problem is to grow them. Scaling implies expanding your revenue without a commensurate increase in work or time. This might involve developing a side company, reinvesting income, or harnessing technology to reach a broader audience.

Expanding company Ventures

If you've launched a side company, look for possibilities to grow. This might mean releasing new items, entering new markets, or expanding your marketing efforts. For example, if you're selling things online, try expanding to other platforms or even overseas markets.In my situation, I began modestly with a few rental houses. As I acquired expertise, I reinvested the earnings to buy other homes and finally transformed from a landlord to a real estate investor managing many properties across various geographies.

Reinvesting Profits

Another successful strategy to increase revenue streams is by reinvesting profits. Whether it's dividends from stocks or rental income, reinvesting may dramatically enhance your wealth over time. Compound interest and the snowball effect are significant instruments for growing passive income. One of the most crucial turning points in my path was when I began reinvesting all my rental revenue into new homes. This method boosted my financial progress and enabled me to expand far quicker than if I had depended simply on my earned income.

Leveraging Technology

Technology may be a game-changer in growing revenue sources. Automation technologies, internet platforms, and digital marketing may help you reach a broader audience and manage your cash sources more effectively. For instance, employing social media advertisements or SEO to generate people for an online company may drastically improve income with minimum added work. I employed technology by putting up automated procedures for my real estate assets, such as online payment systems and maintenance management. This not only reduced time but also enhanced efficiency and profitability.

Letting Your Money Work for You

Automation is the last piece of the jigsaw in developing several revenue streams. By automating your revenue sources, you free up time and energy to concentrate on new possibilities or just enjoy the money you've made.

Automating Investments

Automation in investments may take the shape of automated dividend reinvestment, periodic contributions to retirement accounts, or setting up robo-advisors to manage your portfolio. This guarantees that your money is continually working for you without needing constant attention. When I automated my stock investments, I built up a mechanism where dividends were automatically reinvested into additional shares. This enabled my portfolio to expand steadily without my active engagement, harnessing the potential of compound interest.

Delegating chores

If you're operating a company or managing properties, automating regular chores or delegating them to others may dramatically boost productivity. For example, engaging a property manager to address tenant complaints or utilizing software to monitor rental payments might change an active revenue stream into a more passive one. In my real estate adventure, one of the finest moves I made was to employ a property management business. This decision liberated me from day-to-day duties and put my real estate revenue into a more passive stream, enabling me to concentrate on expanding other projects.

Setting Up regular money

One of the most effective kinds of automation is setting up regular money streams. This might be in the form of subscription services, membership sites, or rental revenue. Recurring revenue delivers regular cash flow with minimum effort, making it simpler to anticipate and manage finances. For instance, when I established an online course, I put it up as a subscription-based business. This not only supplied recurring money but also automated most of the content distribution and client administration, enabling the firm to function smoothly with minimum effort.

Conclusion

Creating several revenue sources is a dynamic and gratifying experience. By identifying prospective sources, balancing active and passive income, increasing your streams, and automating them, you may construct a healthy financial portfolio that supports your road to wealth. The route may have its hurdles, but with persistence and the appropriate techniques, you may attain financial independence and enjoy the freedom that comes with it. I employed technology by putting up automated procedures for my real estate assets, such as online payment systems and maintenance management. This not only reduced time but also enhanced efficiency and profitability.

7

Harnessing the Power of Technology

In today's fast-expanding world, technology is the driving force behind innumerable advances that may dramatically enhance your road toward financial independence. From digital tools that automate revenue streams to cutting-edge innovations like cryptocurrencies and blockchain, learning how to harness the power of technology is vital for anybody trying to manage passive income in the contemporary day. This chapter will lead you through the crucial technical resources that may drive you toward riches.

Digital Tools for Passive Income

Technology has altered the way we approach passive income, giving a variety of digital tools meant to simplify and improve your financial plans. Whether you're managing investments, automating company processes, or even earning revenue online, the appropriate tools may be game-changers.

Investment Management Platforms

Investment management platforms have democratized the world of investing, making it simpler than ever to design and manage a diverse portfolio without having to be a financial expert. Platforms like **Robo-advisors** employ algorithms to manage your investments, automatically rebalancing your portfolio depending on your risk tolerance and financial objectives. These tools enable you to invest with confidence, knowing that your money is being handled properly.

Automation Software

Automation is crucial to expanding passive revenue, and there are several software options available that may assist automate different areas of your company. For example, **email marketing platforms like Mailchimp or ConvertKit enable you to build up automatic email sequences that connect with your audience on autopilot.** Similarly, e-*commerce platforms like Shopify allow you to automate order processing, inventory management, and customer care.*

Digital Payment Solutions

Digital payment options like PayPal, Stripe, and Square have made it simpler than ever to take payments from consumers globally. These systems provide safe and simple methods to handle transactions, whether you're selling things online, freelancing, or operating a subscription business. By integrating these technologies into your organization, you can provide a smooth experience for your consumers while optimizing your cash flow. When I initially created an online course, putting up a dependable payment mechanism was a key concern. I picked PayPal and Stripe for their simplicity of use and broad usage. This approach paid dividends, as it enabled me to reach a worldwide audience and secure timely payments, adding considerably to the course's success.

Budgeting and Expense Tracking Apps
Managing your money successfully is key to growing wealth, and budgeting programs like Mint, YNAB (You Need a Budget), and Personal Capital may be useful tools. These applications let you monitor income, spending, and assets, offering a comprehensive picture of your financial health. They also provide tools like goal setting and progress monitoring, which are vital for anybody serious about obtaining financial independence.

Use a budgeting program to create financial objectives and measure your success. For example, if you're saving for a down payment on a rental property, set a designated savings goal in the app and track your contributions periodically. This keeps you responsible and motivated to attain your objective.

Online Business Models

The internet has opened up a world of possibilities for producing revenue, and knowing the different online business strategies is crucial to capitalizing on these opportunities. From e-commerce to digital goods, internet business concepts provide scalable solutions to build passive revenue streams that may expand exponentially.

E-commerce and Dropshipping

E-commerce is one of the most popular Internet business concepts, enabling you to sell things directly to customers via an online shop. One especially enticing version of e-commerce is **dropshipping**, where you sell things without retaining inventories. When a client makes a purchase, the goods are transported straight from the supplier to the consumer, removing the need for you to handle inventories. To succeed in dropshipping, concentrate on identifying a niche market with strong demand but minimal competition. Use resources like Google Trends and Amazon's Best Sellers list to uncover hot goods. Additionally, verify that your provider is credible and delivers timely shipments to preserve client happiness.

Affiliate Marketing

Affiliate marketing is another effective online business concept that enables you to earn commissions by advertising other people's goods or services. As an affiliate, you may make cash by bringing visitors to a merchant's website using unique affiliate links. You get paid when someone uses your link to make a purchase. To optimize your affiliate marketing efforts, concentrate on providing quality content that answers your audience's problem points. For example, if you're marketing a financial planning tool, write a blog post or make a video that explains how the program may help customers reach their financial objectives. Include your affiliate link in the material to boost conversions.

Digital Products and Courses

Creating and selling digital assets, such as eBooks, online courses, or templates, is a scalable approach to making passive revenue. Once you've built a digital product, it may be sold again without the requirement for inventory or delivery. Online courses, in particular, have become a profitable sector, with platforms like **Udemy, Teachable, and Skillshare** making it easier to reach a worldwide audience. When producing a digital product or course, concentrate on giving outstanding value. Conduct rigorous research to understand your audience's demands and pain spots, and ensure that your solution meets them effectively. Use pre-sales or beta testing to get feedback and perfect your product before selling it to a broader audience.

Cryptocurrency and Blockchain Opportunities

Cryptocurrency and blockchain technology have emerged as innovative inventions with the potential to transform the financial landscape. While they come with hazards, they also offer substantial potential for anyone prepared to explore this new frontier.

Understanding Cryptocurrency

Cryptocurrency is a sort of digital or virtual money that employs cryptography for security. Bitcoin, the first and most well-known cryptocurrency, was launched in 2009 and has since been joined by hundreds of other cryptocurrencies. Unlike conventional currencies, cryptocurrencies run on decentralized networks based on blockchain technology, making them impervious to government control and meddling. I originally got interested in cryptocurrencies during its early years when Bitcoin was still a rather unknown notion. My early investments were tiny since I wanted to test the waters without committing too much funds. Over time, as I developed a greater grasp of the technology and the industry, I increased my investments, which proved to be a lucrative option as the value of cryptocurrencies surged.If you're new to cryptocurrencies, start by educating yourself on the basics. Read whitepapers, follow credible news sources, and join online groups to keep informed. When you're ready to invest, start with a small amount that you can afford to lose, since the market may be quite **volatile**.

Blockchain Technology

Blockchain is the underlying technology that underpins cryptocurrencies. It is a decentralized ledger that records transactions over a network of computers. Blockchain's openness, security, and immutability have made it a transformational force in multiple sectors, from banking to supply chain management.

Opportunities Beyond cryptocurrencies

While blockchain is most usually identified with cryptocurrencies, its uses extend well beyond digital money. For example, smart contracts—self-executing contracts with the contents of the agreement explicitly put into code—have the potential to revolutionize legal arrangements, decreasing the need for intermediaries and enhancing efficiency. To profit on blockchain potential, consider investing in startups with real-world applications and strong development teams. Look for initiatives that have obvious use cases and are tackling critical challenges in their respective industry. Additionally, try diversifying your blockchain assets to mitigate risk.

Navigating the Risks

While the potential returns of cryptocurrency and blockchain ventures are crucial, it's vital to realize the hazards. The market is still very new, and pricing may be quite volatile. Regulatory instability and the possibility for fraud or hacking are further problems that investors must be aware of. To reduce risks, diversify your investing portfolio by include a mix of conventional assets (such as equities and bonds) with cryptocurrency. Consider utilizing safe, reliable exchanges and wallets to protect your valuables. It's also good to be educated on regulatory developments, since changes in government policy may have a substantial influence on the market.

STAYING AHEAD IN A DIGITAL WORLD

In an age of fast technological development, keeping ahead of the curve is vital for preserving and developing your revenue streams. Embracing lifelong learning, adjusting to new trends, and harnessing technology are all vital tactics for succeeding in a digital age.

Embracing Lifelong Learning

The rate of technology innovation implies that the skills and information you have now may become outdated tomorrow. To remain competitive, it's necessary to commit to lifelong learning. This might mean taking online classes, attending seminars, or just keeping up with industry news. Set aside time each week for learning and skill improvement. This might be as easy as reading articles, listening to podcasts, or enrolling in an online course. Focus on topics that are relevant to your present revenue streams or that might open up new possibilities in the future.

Adapting to New Trends

Technology develops swiftly, and those who can adapt to new trends are frequently the ones that win. This involves being open to experimenting with new technologies, platforms, and business strategies. Whether it's adopting a new social media platform to engage your audience or investigating the possibilities of artificial intelligence in your organization, being flexible is key. Keep an eye on developing technology and trends in your sector. Follow think leaders, attend conferences, and engage in online forums to keep informed. When you uncover a potential trend, explore how it may be implemented into your company or investing plan.

Leveraging Technology for Efficiency

One of the main benefits of technology is its capacity to boost efficiency. By embracing digital solutions, you may simplify processes, decrease expenses, and increase your revenue sources more efficiently. This can entail automating processes, leveraging data analytics to make educated choices, or deploying cloud-based solutions to boost cooperation. Regularly examine your existing tools and procedures to discover places where technology might increase efficiency. This might require updating software, integrating new technologies, or adopting more complex analytics. The objective is to establish a simplified process that increases production while eliminating wasted time and resources.

Conclusion

Harnessing the power of technology is not simply a choice; it's a need for anybody serious about reaching financial independence in today's digital environment. By embracing digital technologies, investigating online business ideas, tapping into cryptocurrency and blockchain possibilities, and keeping ahead of technical changes, you can establish a comprehensive, future-proof plan for earning and maintaining passive income. Embrace the opportunities that technology brings, and you'll find yourself well-equipped to traverse the route to riches.

8

Overcoming Challenges and Setbacks

In every road toward financial freedom, obstacles and disappointments are inevitable. The route to success is not always easy, but it is these hurdles that develop our character and create our resilience. This chapter will discuss frequent hazards, how to learn from financial blunders, the necessity of keeping motivated during challenging times, and tactics for developing resilience and flexibility.

Common Pitfalls and How to Avoid Them

When attaining financial freedom, various traps might impede your progress. Being aware of these typical pitfalls and learning how to avoid them is vital to remaining on track.

Overestimating Your Income Potential

One of the most frequent errors individuals make is overestimating their earning potential, especially in the early phases of developing passive income streams. It's tempting to get caught up in the enthusiasm of a new investment or business endeavor and expect it will start providing considerable revenue right soon. However, this approach may lead to disappointment and irritation when outcomes don't reach expectations. Always approach new revenue sources with cautious confidence. Do your due homework, develop cautious financial estimates, and include a cushion in your budget for unanticipated costs.

This way, you won't be taken off guard if things don't go as planned.

Ignoring Risk Management

Another danger is disregarding the necessity of risk management. Whether it's an investment in the stock market, real estate, or a new business endeavor, every opportunity comes with risk. Failing to recognize and minimize these risks may lead to considerable financial losses.Diversify your assets across multiple asset types to spread risk. Additionally, consider establishing stop-loss orders on your assets to reduce future losses. Regularly examine your portfolio and make modifications as required to match your risk tolerance and financial objectives.

Learning from Financial Mistakes

Mistakes are an unavoidable part of the financial path. However, the key to success rests not in avoiding errors completely, but in learning from them and applying those lessons to make better judgments in the future.

Embracing Failure as a Learning Opportunity

It's easy to feel discouraged after a financial loss, but it's crucial to consider failure as a learning opportunity rather than a dead end. Every mistake you make delivers vital lessons that may influence your future actions. After the stock market loss I discussed before, I was crushed. I questioned my capacity to make wise financial judgments and even pondered giving up on my goal of financial freedom. However, after meditating on the event, I recognized that this setback was a chance to learn and improve. I began researching risk management tactics and made it a point to diversify my investments going forward. This adjustment in perspective helped me recover from the loss and eventually become a more confident and educated investor. Whenever you make a financial error, take the time to understand what went wrong and why. Write out the major lessons you've learned and how you intend to use them in the future. This exercise not only helps you avoid making the same errors but also fosters a development mentality that will serve you well in many aspects of life.

Using Setbacks to Refine Your Strategy

Setbacks may sometimes be beneficial in helping you modify your financial approach. Sometimes, a setback is an indication that a specific method isn't working and has to be modified. At one time, I recognized that my real estate investments were not producing the profits I had hoped for. The homes needed more care than projected, and the rental market in the region had become saturated. Instead of continuing to pump money into these properties, I opted to sell them and reinvest in a new area with more development prospects. This choice finally resulted in a big boost in my total results. Don't be scared to pivot when something isn't working. Be ready to let go of failing assets or methods and investigate other options that correspond better with your financial objectives. Flexibility and adaptation are important to long-term success.

Staying Motivated During Tough Times

The route to financial freedom may be long and arduous, and it's easy to lose motivation when things go rough. However, keeping your motivation is vital for remaining on track and completing your objectives.

Keeping Your 'Why' in Focus

One of the most effective methods to remain motivated is to maintain your 'why'—your purpose for attaining financial independence—at the forefront of your thoughts. Whether it's the desire for greater independence, the capacity to spend more time with family, or the aim of leaving a legacy, having a strong 'why' will keep you going even when the going gets rough. During the early years of my trip, there were numerous instances when I felt like giving up. The sacrifices, the disappointments, and the uncertainty frequently made me doubt if it was all worth it. But every time I felt like quitting, I reminded myself of my 'why'—the vision I had for my life and the freedom I wanted to accomplish. This kept me motivated and helped me push through the tough periods. Write down your 'why' and set it someplace you'll see it every day, such as on your bathroom mirror or in your wallet. This regular reminder can help you remain focused and motivated, even when confronted with problems.

Celebrating Small Wins
Another great method to retain motivation is to celebrate tiny accomplishments along the road. Recognizing and recognizing your success, no matter how modest, may raise your morale and keep you going ahead. I made it a point to celebrate every milestone, no matter how tiny. Whether it was paying off a credit card, meeting a savings target, or finishing a profitable real estate purchase, I took the time to recognize and thank myself for the progress I was making. These tiny festivities helped keep my spirits up and reaffirmed the sense that I was on the right course. Set up tiny, realistic

benchmarks on your route to financial freedom. When you hit a milestone, celebrate in a meaningful manner, whether it's treating yourself to something special or just taking the time to reflect on your accomplishments. These modest celebrations can help you remain optimistic and inspired.

Building Resilience and Adaptability

Resilience and flexibility are two of the most crucial skills you can build on your journey to financial freedom. The capacity to bounce back from failures and adapt to changing circumstances is vital for long-term success.

Developing a Growth Mindset

Resilience starts with a growth mindset—the conviction that difficulties and failures are opportunities for progress rather than barriers to be avoided. With a growth mentality, you'll be better able to manage hardship and transform it into a stepping stone for future achievement.Cultivate a growth mentality by concentrating on the lessons you can gain from each situation, rather than dwelling on the disadvantages. Embrace obstacles as chances to learn and grow, and you'll find yourself growing more resilient over time.

Being Open to Change

Adaptability is another crucial component of resilience. The financial world is continuously changing, and being open to change is vital for keeping ahead. Whether it's adjusting to new market conditions, changing rules, or alterations in your circumstances, being adaptable and prepared to modify your plan is vital for long-term success. There were instances when I had to make big modifications to my financial plan owing to unanticipated occurrences, such as market downturns or personal issues. Rather than opposing change, I learned to welcome it and alter my approach as required. This agility helped me to manage hurdles more successfully and finally attain my financial objectives. Regularly examine your financial plan and be open to making modifications when required. Stay updated about changes in the industry and be open to investigating new possibilities or revisiting old ones with a fresh perspective. By being adaptive, you'll be better ready to face whatever problems come your way.

Conclusion

Overcoming hurdles and disappointments is an unavoidable aspect of the route to financial freedom. By being aware of frequent errors, learning from mistakes, keeping motivated, and creating resilience and flexibility, you may convert hurdles into chances for progress. Remember, the route to wealth is not a straight line, but with persistence, adaptability, and a positive outlook, you can negotiate the twists and turns and emerge stronger on the other side.

9

The Psychology of Wealth Building

The route to financial freedom starts in the head. Developing a wealth mentality is not simply about thinking optimistically or wishing for success—it's about adopting a set of beliefs, attitudes, and actions that correspond with the aims of wealth building. When I initially began my journey to financial freedom, I learned that my ideas were my largest impediment. I had to unlearn the scarcity attitude implanted in me and replace it with an abundance mentality. A wealth mentality is about finding opportunities where others perceive problems. It's about realizing that money is not only a matter of chance but a product of constant work, smart thinking, **and a willingness to take measured risks.** In my early days, I battled criticism and uncertainty, both

from others and inside myself. However, by intentionally choosing to concentrate on development, learning, and resilience, I transformed my viewpoint. Instead of asking, "Why me?" When confronted with problems, I started asking, "What can I learn from this?" Cultivating a wealth mentality also includes surrounding oneself with good influencers. I began reading books by successful entrepreneurs, attending seminars, and networking with like-minded folks who had attained financial freedom. This exposure allowed me to imagine broader and dream braver. It's vital to remember that your mentality will either be your greatest advantage or your largest hindrance on your trip. Choose to perceive the opportunities, and you'll find yourself on the proper road to riches.

Habits' Significance for Financial Achievement

Habits are the basis upon which prosperity is created. While large concepts and huge ideas are necessary, it's the everyday, consistent activities that ultimately lead to financial success. Early in my trip, I learned that simple, apparently trivial behaviors may either drive me ahead or keep me back. **For instance, the practice of documenting every expenditure, no matter how tiny, gave me control over my money.** It's easy to underestimate how much those daily coffees or impulsive purchases pile up, but when you monitor everything, you become more mindful of your spending. One of the practices that had the most significant influence on my financial success was saving away a percentage of my salary for investments before spending on anything else. This behavior, commonly referred to as **"paying yourself first,"** guaranteed that I was continually accumulating my money, regardless of how much I made. Over time, this basic behavior accumulated, resulting in a tremendous increase in my investment account. But habits are not only about what you do—they're about how you think. Developing the practice of thinking long-term, for instance, helped me avoid the desire to seek rapid, short-term advantages. Instead, I concentrated on tactics that would bring sustainable development over time. Remember, your financial performance is a mirror of your everyday behaviors. By persistently following the behaviors that fit with your financial objectives, you'll gradually but surely create the money you seek.

Visualization and Goal-Setting Techniques

Visualization and goal planning are essential instruments in the wealth-building process. They give direction, motivation, and a clear vision of what you want to accomplish. Early in my voyage, I learned that without a defined aim, I was merely wandering. It wasn't until I sat down and clearly defined what financial freedom meant to me that I started to make actual progress. I envisioned what my life would look like after I reached my goals—what my days would be like, where I would live, and how I would spend my time. This mental image proved a great motivator, particularly during challenging times. Goal setting is the practical part of this process. It's about breaking down your vision into actionable actions. I began by creating both short-term and long-term objectives, making sure each one was precise, measurable, attainable, relevant, and time-bound (SMART). For instance, instead of loosely declaring, "I want to be financially independent," I established a goal to construct a portfolio that provides money in passive income per month within three years. This precision made my aims concrete and gave me a clear route to follow. One strategy that worked well for me was reverse engineering my objectives. I began with the destination in mind and proceeded backward, identifying the steps required to get there. This technique not only made the procedure less intimidating but also enabled me to monitor my progress more efficiently. Visualization and goal setting are not just about dreaming—they're about building a clear, concrete strategy that drives you toward financial freedom.

The Impact of Community and Networking

No one earns money in solitude. The people you surround yourself with may have a dramatic influence on your financial success. Early in my journey, I understood that I needed to develop a network of supportive, like-minded folks who shared my aims and desires. This wasn't always easy—there were moments when I felt like I was swimming against the flow, particularly when many around me didn't understand my goal for financial freedom. But I continued, searching out organizations and networks that might give me the support and assistance I needed. One of the most essential things I learned was the significance of giving as much as you get in these networks. By sharing my expertise and experiences, I not only assisted others but also increased my grasp of wealth-building ideas. Networking also provided doors to possibilities I would never have explored on my own. Whether it was a fresh investment possibility, a prospective collaboration, or just a piece of advice that altered my viewpoint, these relationships were vital. The influence of community and networking extends beyond only opportunities—it also gives responsibility and incentives. Being part of a group of individuals who are all working towards similar objectives keeps you focused and pushed. When you witness others achieve their objectives, it strengthens the confidence that you can too. Remember, your network is your net worth. Surround yourself with people who raise you, push you, and encourage you, and you'll find the route to financial independence much more enjoyable and feasible. By concentrating on these aspects—developing a wealth mentality, creating productive habits, employing visualization and goal planning, and using the power of community and networking—you create the psychological basis for financial success. These aspects work together to keep you motivated, focused, and resilient, even in the face of obstacles.Remember that the attitude you create, the habits you establish, and the people you surround yourself with will play a key influence in your capacity to attain financial independence.

10

Living Your Financially Independent Life

Reaching financial independence is a monumental achievement, but it's important to recognize that this milestone is not the end—it's the beginning of a new chapter in life. As I approached financial independence, I realized that my definition of success began to shift. It was no longer just about numbers in a bank account or the size of my investment portfolio. Instead, success became about living a life that aligned with my values, passions, and the relationships that mattered most to me. Happiness, I found, isn't something that magically appears when you achieve financial independence. It's something you cultivate along the way. For years, I chased financial goals, thinking that once I hit a certain number, I would finally feel fulfilled. But the truth is, happiness is more about the journey than the destination.

THE PASSIVE PATH TO PROSPERITY

It's about finding joy in the everyday moments—spending time with loved ones, pursuing passions, and contributing to causes that matter to you. Financial independence gives you the freedom to redefine what success and happiness mean on your terms. For me, it meant shifting my focus from accumulating wealth to enjoying life's experiences and making a positive impact on others. It's about waking up every day with a sense of purpose and fulfillment, knowing that you have the freedom to choose how you spend your time. As you reach this stage in your journey, take the time to reflect on what truly makes you happy and redefine your vision of success beyond financial metrics.

Giving Back

The Joy of Philanthropy

One of the most fulfilling aspects of financial independence is the ability to give back. Reaching my financial goals, I realized that true wealth isn't just about what you have—it's about what you can give. Philanthropy became a significant part of my life, and I found immense joy in using my resources to support causes and communities that I care about. Giving back isn't just about writing a check or making a donation. It's about investing your time, energy, and resources in ways that make a meaningful impact. For me, this meant mentoring aspiring entrepreneurs, supporting educational initiatives, and contributing to organizations that align with my values. These experiences not only allowed me to give back but also enriched my life in ways I hadn't anticipated.Philanthropy also provided a sense of purpose that went beyond my personal financial goals. It reminded me that wealth comes with responsibility—the responsibility to use it wisely and for the greater good. I encourage you to explore the causes that resonate with you and find ways to give back. Whether it's through financial contributions, volunteering, or sharing your knowledge and skills, giving back can bring immense joy and fulfillment, enriching both your life and the lives of others.

Planning for a Legacy

As you build wealth and achieve financial independence, it's natural to start thinking about the legacy you want to leave behind. For me, legacy planning became a crucial part of my financial journey, as I wanted to ensure that the wealth I created would continue to have a positive impact long after I was gone.Planning for a legacy involves more than just estate planning or deciding who inherits your assets. It's about thinking deeply about the values, principles, and lessons you want to pass on to future generations. I spent time reflecting on the experiences that shaped my financial journey—the challenges I overcame, the lessons I learned, and the values that guided my decisions. I wanted these to be part of the legacy I left behind, not just the financial assets. Creating a legacy plan also means making intentional decisions about how your wealth will be used in the future. For some, this might involve setting up a trust or foundation to support charitable causes, while for others, it might mean ensuring that family members are equipped with the financial knowledge and resources they need to succeed. Whatever your approach, planning for a legacy is about making sure that your wealth continues to create value, even when you're no longer here to guide it.

Continuous Growth and Learning

Financial independence is not the end of the road—it's the beginning of a new journey. One of the most important lessons I've learned is that growth and learning are continuous processes. Even after achieving financial independence, I committed to keep challenging myself, learning new skills, and exploring new opportunities.The world is constantly changing, and staying ahead requires a mindset of continuous growth. For me, this meant staying curious, seeking out new knowledge, and remaining open to new ideas. Whether it was learning about new investment opportunities, exploring emerging technologies, or expanding my understanding of global markets, I realized that continuous learning was key to maintaining and growing my wealth.But growth isn't just about financial knowledge. It's also about personal development—improving your mindset, health, and relationships. I made it a point to invest in myself, whether through personal coaching, attending seminars, or simply reading books that challenged my perspectives. This commitment to growth helped me stay adaptable and resilient, no matter what challenges came my way. As you embark on this new chapter of financial independence, I encourage you to embrace a mindset of continuous growth and learning. Keep pushing your boundaries, stay curious, and never stop exploring new possibilities. By doing so, you'll ensure that your financial independence is not just a destination but a journey of lifelong growth and fulfillment. In living your financially independent life, remember that it's about more than just the freedom to do what you want. It's about redefining success, giving back to others, planning a lasting legacy, and committing to continuous growth. These principles will not only help you maintain your financial independence but also enrich your life in ways that go far beyond money.

www.ingramcontent.com/pod-product-compliance
Lightning Source LLC
Chambersburg PA
CBHW050308230526
45471CB00005B/2086